Just Setters

Just Setters

TEXT BY STEVE SMITH

WILLOW CREEK PRESS

MINOCQUA, WISCONSIN

Published by Willow Creek Press
P.O. Box 147
Minocqua, Wisconsin 54548

Designed by Heather M. McElwain

For information on other Willow Creek titles,
call 1-800-850-9453

Library of Congress Cataloging-in-Publication Data

Smith, Steve.
   Just setters / text by Steve Smith.
      p.   cm.
   ISBN 1-57223-178-5
   1. Setters (Dogs) 2. Setters (Dogs)--Pictorial works.
I. Title.
   SF429.S5S55   1998
   636.752'6--dc21   98-39316
                         CIP

Printed in Canada

PHOTOGRAPHY CREDITS

Jeff Druckrey: page 2; Mark Raycroft: pages 6, 12, 17, 19, 20-21, 23, 42 (bottom right), 43, 55, and 63; Dale C. Spartas: pages 7, 8, 9, 25, 28 (top), 30, 33, 38, 39, 40, 42 (top), 45, 51 (right), 54, 56 (right), 58, 59 (both), 60 (all), 61, 74, 76, 77, 81, 83 (left), 84, 86, 87 (all), 93 (both), 94 (left), 97 (top right), 99 (top left), 100, 102 (right), 103, 106 (bottom right), 111 (top & bottom right), 112 (left), 113, 122, 123 (top), 124 (all), 125, 127 (bottom), 128 (both), 129, 130, 134, 138 (left & bottom right), 140, 141 (all), 142, and 143; John Schafer: pages 4-5, 10, 63 (all), 68 (both), 70 (all), 71, 104 (right), 120, 127 (top), 131, and 135 (left); Ron Kimball: pages 13, 36, 108 (right), and 116; Sharon Eide / S & E Photo: pages 14, 31, 32, 41, 47, and 135 (right); Elizabeth Flynn / S & E Photo: page 15; Kent and Donna Dannen: pages 16, 18, 24, 26, 27, 28 (bottom), 29, 35, 42 (bottom left), 50 (right), 65 (top right), 69, 72 (top & bottom right), 73, 75, 121, 123 (bottom), 126, and 133; IFA/Uniphoto: page 22; Denver Bryan: pages 34, 37, 85 (top & bottom right), 90, 92, 94 (bottom right), and 105 (right); Donald D. Carey: page 46; Alan & Sandy Carey: page 51 (left); Tom Davis: pages 48, 53, 72 (bottom left), 94 (center right), 136 (both), and 134 (top right); Walter Cottrell: pages 49, 117, 118-119, and 144; Ron Spomer: pages 50 (left), 56 (left), 57, 62 (left), 78-79, 80 (left), 85 (bottom left), 88, 89, 91, 96, 97 (bottom left), 98, 102 (left & center), 104, 105 (left), 106 (top & bottom left), 107, 108, 109 (left), 111 (left), 114, 132, and 139; Jean Wentworth: pages 52, 64, and 137; Jason Smith: page 62 (right); Bonnie Nance: pages 66; Dave Meisner: pages 80 (right), 94 (top right), 99 (bottom right), and 101; Bill Buckley / Green Agency: pages 82, 83 (right), 95, and 110; David Bitters: page 115.

Contents

For Jess and Sadie

Introduction

Setters: Many Faces, Many Moods

I'VE SPENT A GOOD PORTION OF MY ADULT LIFE LIVING WITH SETTERS, PARTICULARLY English setters, and I am here to tell you that they are frauds. They look so elegant, so well bred, so aristocratic, but it's all just a pretty good scam.

Scratch a setter – English, Irish, or Gordon – and you'll find a mutt, a mutt that digs up your tulip bulbs, sleeps on the furniture, begs from the table, opens the neighbors' garbage bags, terrorizes the local kitty-cats, and generally acts like a hooligan.

Oh, they do a few other things as well. If there is anything in the canine world more beautiful than an English, Irish, or Gordon setter coursing a field, the wind blowing those long, feathery locks, I don't know what it is. If there is a more faithful, loving, protective companion, I'm not sure what it would be. And nowhere will you see a more astute, perceptive student of the human condition than a setter. They know our moods, and they alter theirs to harmonize with them.

One thing that has always fascinated me is watching dogs dream. Dogs are creatures who are not supposed to be capable of rational thought in the way you and I are. If that's the case – and I don't happen to believe it is – how can we say that they are capable of dreaming, which it seems would require imagination? Anyone who has spent any time with dogs knows that they do indeed dream, and setters are the worst (best?) dreamers because they seem to sleep a lot more than other breeds.

My setters live with me. They usually plant themselves under my desk and crowd my feet when I'm trying to work, or they take turns sleeping in the big chair in my office, the one I keep covered so that if someone who wants to talk drops over, I can offer him a sort of hairless place to sit. Not that it does much good. About the time that Jess and Parker figure out the visitor is a friend worth knowing, they give him the setter welcome and his clothes end up looking like who-finished-second in the pillow fight.

Lately, my relatives have started to talk about me and my setters behind our backs. The reason is, I think, because I talk to them. All the time. They hardly ever answer except to smile with their tails, but they know when I've had a bad day and try to cheer me up with a paw in my lap, a quick kiss on the cheek, or a head on my knee.

When I've had a particularly horrible day, my older dog, Jess, has been known, on occasion, to join me for a nip from the Company Bottle of Scotch. Jess likes a good single-malt Scotch and water, and a couple of cubes to chew on when she's finished.

Some breeds are considered one-person dogs, setters adopt the whole family. When my son Chris was younger, he got sick and was bed-ridden for a couple of days. The dogs watched over him in shifts from the foot of his bed. Not sleeping, really, just curled up, resting, with their eyes open watching him and

listening to his breathing, adding the warmth of an orange-ticked body to the blankets to ward off the chills of fever and the bad things that can stalk young children in the darkness.

Neither dog could be coaxed from the bedroom. They would alternate watches. Parker would walk down the hallway to Chris' room, give an unspoken yet understood signal to Jess, who would hop off the bed while Parker hopped on. Jess would then go get a drink or take a bite from her dish, or go outside for a stroll. An hour later, she'd go relieve Parker. This went on day and night for three days until the antibiotics worked and the boy got better. Nothing could alter their watching and listening and changing of the guard until he was well.

I know some people who think of dogs as servants, to do for us those things we cannot do for ourselves, using their exceptional senses and willing-ness to please, to be at our beck and call. Our setters are our friends, not our possessions, and they are never closer to us than when they do something extraordinary, even if its chasing an unseen bird or conjured cat or running off an imaginary intruder in their sleep. Bless their dreams.

This book is for them, the dogs of England, Ireland, and Scotland who across the years and across the miles have brought so much joy to so many of us.

– Steve Smith
Traverse City, Michigan

Portraits:
The Irish Setter

Forever Young

WE KNOW THE IRISH SETTER TODAY AS A BIG, LONG, LANKY, DOG WITH flowing locks and the narrow head, one of the most singularly beautiful dogs on earth. Good friends of mine own such an Irish. Barney – for this is the name of the beast – is as faithful, loving, and gentle as any animal I have ever seen, despite his hundred-plus pounds. He is fast friends with one of the family's other dogs, a Jack Russell terrier named Milo, who weighs less than a tenth of what Barney does, yet possesses the fabled Jack Russell brains. Milo does all the thinking for them. Though Barney, a pliable enough sort,

could crush the little fellow with a single bite, he instead follows the smaller dog's lead. If there ever was a canine Odd Couple, they are it.

The original, true Irish setter – developed, as you have no doubt deduced, in Ireland – was and still is in some quarters a rough and tumble bird dog. Marked with the familiar red, it also carries a good amount of white. Although its genesis as a breed is shrouded in the same mists of time that swirl around many of the recognized breeds, the theory the AKC seems to accept is that the Irish setter is an "English setter-spaniel-pointer combination with a dash of Gordon thrown in."

"Red setters," becoming popular in North America, have a lot of Irish blood in them, as well as that of English setters (part of the breeding program for these dogs is to periodically "outcross," breeding to English setters). The resultant pups are then bred back into the red setter line, and the pups from those breedings bred back to still other red setters. This way, the English

setter's looks all but disappear, while much of the nose and hunting instinct remain. But such linebreedings over time diminish the Englishman's nose in the red dogs, and so the outcrossings take place again, and the whole cycle repeats. Red setter breeders feel that this breeding method will eventually instill a high-quality nose in their dogs, and outcrosses will no longer be necessary. I have hunted with red dogs, and as soon as I can get someone to part with a pup, I'll have one. But there's a long waiting list, and breeders are few.

Even though Irish setters around the turn of the last century were gun dogs of the highest caliber on both sides of the Atlantic, in this country their beauty was their undoing, at least as sporting companions. Bred for the show ring, they emerged as big, beautiful animals with absolutely no sporting instincts whatsoever, and as some of the breed's critics say, its particular intellectual star shines with somewhat reduced brilliance. Where English setters are often

described as "intelligent and friendly," and Gordons are said to be "intelligent, friendly, and loyal," Irish setters are often said to be "lively and affectionate."

But that has not attenuated their nature as loving animals that live for affection from their owners. In fact, their need for love and contact often overwhelms the contactee, who finds that ignoring a high-spirited Irishman intent on getting petted and hugged is like ignoring the oncoming five-fifteen headed for Hartford with your car stalled across the tracks: You can do it for a little while, but eventually it becomes impossible.

That's why those who have give their hearts to these dogs say that the puppiness never quite leaves them, that they will seemingly be pups their entire lives.

The Irish setter of today is – with individual exceptions – a loyal companion, a lovable schmo with the beauty to light up a room and the personality to match. To those for whom the adoration is mutual, that's quite enough.

Portraits:
The Gordon Setter

Aristocracy's Gift

I T IS SAID THAT THE GORDON SETTER WAS DEVELOPED IN SCOTLAND BY ALEXANDER, the Fourth Duke of Gordon, in the 18th century, hence the name. But the reality is that there were probably nearly a dozen wealthy Scottish sportsmen breeding what were then called "black and tan setters" at about the same time. This takes nothing away from the Duke's devotion to the breed, however, and it is said that so many Scots liked to claim they owned one of "Gordon's setters" that the name was officially changed by the Kennel Club of Great Britain to Gordon setter in 1924. Plus, in the status-conscious British Isles, it didn't

hurt your cause to have a noble name attached to the object of your affection.

These dogs, like the other setters, are a favorite of those who breed for the show ring, but they have their staunch supporters among the sporting public as well. I know one conclave of Gordon setter owners who get together every fall in the Bitterroot Mountains of northwestern Montana for a week-long ruffed grouse hunt. The talent these animals display in finding and pointing the elusive grouse is nothing short of astonishing. The friends admire each other's dogs, buy, sell, and swap promising pups, and generally have a grand time. And if a couple of the females head back home in "a family way," oh well.

The black-and-tan coloration of this breed, however, makes them difficult to see in heavy woodland cover, and most serious bird hunters choose the easier-to-see English setter with its

overall white appearance. That's too bad, because those Gordons I have seen in the field give nothing away to any of the pointing breeds when it comes to the work they love so well.

Gordons are known to be brainy animals as dogs go, perhaps the smartest of the three breeds of setters. If you could talk to all of them and posed the question: "What is the largest city in Louisiana?" the Irish setter would say "North Dakota," and then try to wrestle you to the floor.

The English setter would rouse from a nap, yawn, and reply: "New Orleans."

The Gordon would look at you as though you just fell off the turnip truck and say, "New Orleans, naturally. But the capital, of course, is Baton Rouge."

Portraits:
The English Setter

The Keeper of the Flame

ENGLISH SETTERS ARE THE PATRIARCHS OF THE SETTER CLAN. MORE THAN 400 years ago, in England, they were being used by sportsmen to point game for the nets or the hawk. It's possible that the breed originated from the Spanish pointer, large water spaniel, and springer spaniel; others maintain that there is no pointer involved and that the setter is an improved setting spaniel, a descendant of a spaniel quite different from those of today. But no one really knows for sure. Like so many breeds, it came to us after a pinch of this and a dash of that, and who is really responsible and how they did it is often a matter of conjecture.

Quoting here from *Sporting Dogs Recognized by the American Kennel Club: An Official Publication, 1935:*

"There is little doubt that the major credit for the development of the modern [English] setter should go to Mr. Edward Lavarack, who about 1825 obtained from the Rev. A. Harrison, "Ponto" and "Old Moll." The Rev. Harrison had apparently kept their breed pure for thirty-five years or more. From these two setters Mr. Lavarack through a remarkable process of inbreeding, produced by Prince, Countess, Nellie, and Fairy, who were marvelous specimens of English Setters. Along about 1874 Mr. Lavarack sold a pair of dogs to Charles H. Raymond of Morris Plains, New Jersey. During the next ten years the English Setter became more and more popular and it was around this time that many setters bred by Mr. Llewellin were imported into this country and Canada [from England].

"In considering the so-called Llewellin strain it is recorded in the writings of Dr. William A. Brunette that about the time the Lavarack strain of setters was at its zenith in England, Mr. R.L. Purcell Llewellin purchased a number of Mr. Lavarack's

best show dogs of the pure Dash-Moll and Dash-Hill blood, which he obtained in the north of England, represented by Mr. Statter's and Sir Vincent Corbet's strain, since referred to as the Duke-Rhoebes, the latter being the two most prominent members of the blood. The result of these crosses was eminently successful, particularly at field trials, and swept everything before them. Their reputation spread to America and many were purchased by sportsmen in different sections of the United States and Canada, so that this line of breeding soon became firmly established in this country.

"Probably the name that stands out the most conspicuously in the foundation of the field-trial [Llewellin] setter in America is Count Noble. This dog was purchased from Mr. Llewellin by Dave Sanborn of Dowling, Michigan, who, after trying him out on the prairies, was upon the point of returning him to England, but was persuaded not to do so by the late B.F. Wilson of Pittsburgh. On the death of Mr. Sanborn, Count passed into the hands of Mr. Wilson, who gave him an opportunity to demonstrate his sterling qualities from coast to coast. The body

of the famous dog was mounted at his death and is now in the Carnegie Museum at Pittsburgh where it is visited annually by many sportsmen. . . .

". . . The name [Llewellin] was originated in America by breeders who imported dogs from Mr. Llewellin's kennels and, being great admirers of the man and the dogs he bred, they naturally gave them the name of him from whom they were purchased."

It should be noted that the "Llewellin strain" is, in the opinion of many, and with much justification, a true breed of setter. As much work, thought, devotion, and ingenuity – perhaps more – has gone into developing these dogs as went into originating English setters as a breed.

But, because of its various strains and lines, the English setter of today can be a flowing-feathered, bushy-tailed aristocratic show dog; a heavy-jowled, droopy-flewed, chisel-headed New England grouse and woodcock dog; or a thirty-pound, hyperactive, pointy-headed little Coke-bottle-licker Southern quail-finding machine. They are dogs of myriad shapes and styles, bred this way and that for whatever purpose seemed like a good idea at a time.

In terms of color, the most common English setters today are orange beltons (orange markings on a white background), blue beltons (black on white), and tri-colors (both orange and black on white).

Regardless of color, strain, or line, English setters – at least once they are past the puppy stage – are ghosts in the house, given to spending a lot of quiet time by themselves, contemplating who-knows-what, spending perhaps twenty-three hours a day sleeping and the remaining hour eating or begging for food or asking to go outside. That is, unless you have one of those other types of setters who can't stand to be without you, to have you out of their sight, and whose idea of the perfect place to be is in your lap, and it doesn't matter, at least to the dog, if it weighs seventy-five pounds.

In the United States, the first dog ever registered by the American Kennel Club was Adonis, an English setter who was registered in 1878. With a background such as this, you would naturally expect a dog of regal bearing, and of course you'd be right – the average English setter past the puppy stage looks like he or she should be wearing a necktie. But don't be misled – under all is an animal with a sense of humor and a yen for mischief.

Living with Setters

Wherever You Go, Whatever You Do

SETTERS ARE A DEMANDING LOT. THEY DEMAND OUR LOVE, WHICH THEY RETURN in the twinkling of a droopy eye and the flagging of a feathered tail when we enter the room. They demand to know that we are thinking of them, because they are most often thinking of us, possibly because they see us as the Keepers of the Good Times, the ones from whom all good things flow.

Sometimes, though, they are meditative housemates, keeping to themselves, aloof and distant, as though they have important matters to think about and can't be bothered with us. At other times, they seem to relish the contest they see between them and us, a friendly jousting of wills. Sometimes vain and intractable, they use the hours that you and I are off working to lie around and think up things we can do for them.

CLASS. *noun.* Syn.: flair, style, hierarchy, setter.

No matter how we happen to feel some days – or how frumpy or formal our wardrobe choices – a little time with a setter can make us feel elegant. Class – it's hard to define, but we know it when we see it.

Setters are at home as supervisor, observer, and co-conspirator in hour human antics and activities, there to make sure we don't go too far, and to lend a helping paw where needed. They also have a way about them that makes us feel they're evaluating and judging what we do, so we always feel a little relieved and content when they're pleased with us.

S etters of all three breeds will insist that you take them along with you on any little trip you have planned. And if you don't, they take it personally. A friend of mine once made the mistake of locking his keys in his car – along with his English setter. He watched, shouting every threat he could think of while the dog calmly looked at him out of the corner of her eye and ate his steering wheel.

Kids, of course, are the setter's best friends because they are always doing something, always moving. They also usually have on them food or the remnants of their last meal, and what dog could resist the chance for a little lick?

Although setters are not especially noted for being good watchdogs, people who have invited them into their homes know otherwise. Their remarkable hearing and noses are constantly alert to unfamiliar noises and scents, even when they seem to be sound asleep, and they are gallant in defense of their people. Especially kids.

But that doesn't mean, for all their often-contrived stateliness, that they are above a little clowning now and then, especially if it seems to make us happy – and make them the center of attention.

It is not really coincidence to anyone who lives with them that setter rhymes with shedder. On any given day, there is enough setter hair shed in this country to crochet an afghan large enough to cover the infield at Yankee Stadium. So, knowing how fastidious these dogs are when it comes to matters of appearance, you may have to help them out with a little brushing now and then. Perhaps a pedicure to keep those nails looking just right. And as for oral hygiene . . .

A nd if indeed it's true that *setter, thy name is vanity . . .*

. . . then the beauty these animals wear like a cloak justifies their carriage and disposition.

Because as someone once said, "If you've got it, flaunt it."

Hunter, show dog, guardian, companion, confidant, and friend. Those of us who live with setters know they're all of these. And more.

I t is doubtful that any breed enjoys retirement more than a setter. They appear to be in semi-
retirement most of the time anyway, but they accept the advancing years better than other dogs,
realizing that they just may no longer be pups. Certainly they accept it better than we can accept it in
them. Or in ourselves. But they have their memories of youth to keep them warm, the way we all do.

To Seek, Find and Point

What It's All About

Setters are among the most popular hunting breeds in North America. Their style, nose, drive, and willingness to please, and to enter into a productive partnership with a human, has endeared them to legions of bird hunters. And setters are adaptable to most any kind of terrain or game bird, which is why you'll find them hunting anywhere from New England forests to midwestern cornfields, from the prairies of the West to the peafield corners of the South.

E nglish, Gordon, and red setters – in the marrow of their bones, in their blood and spirit, they are all hunters.

Hunting with a setter is like fly-fishing. If the fish aren't cooperating, the fly-fisherman can admire and enjoy his casting. If there are no birds around, the setter owner can delight in watching his dog work. This is not the same dog that snoozes away the day on the furniture back home. This dog is a breed apart.

Because setters love to run, handlers have come up with a variety of tools and techniques to maintain contact and exert their guidance and control over them. Often, more effective than any bells or whistles, the best device is the dog's name screeched with all the stops tied down.

Pigs and fox terriers and collies have been taught to point. Bird dogs – especially setters – do it by instinct and with great style. Setters point the game that their wonderful noses have told them is nearby. In hunting setters, the urge to point overwhelms nearly all else. All canines – wolves and coyotes, for example – stalk and pounce, hesitating before the final leap. Selective breeding and training have refined the hesitation to a pause that can last many minutes. The point tells the dog's human partner that there is game in the vicinity and, in fact, it is *right there.*

The various breeds and strains of setters all had their start as sporting dogs, aiding in the hunting of birds with nets or with hawks. Upon pointing the bird, they would flatten out, stay put, or in some manner "set" until the net was placed somewhere over the bird, and then the dog would flush the bird up and into the net. When used to assist a falconer, the dog's point would alert the raptor and its human partner to the presence of game and then "set" when the bird flushed. Falconers today employ the same techniques.

When shooting became popular in Britain as a means of taking birds in the air, dogs were trained to drop to the sight of a bird on the wing or the sound of a shot. This kept the dog out of any danger of being injured (the game birds of Britain are low flyers due to the low-growth cover they inhabit). In addition, in the early days of sporting firearms, the single-shot shotguns took some time to reload, and a dog that moved out immediately after the shot could flush other birds before the shooter was ready, so all that "setting" business made sense.

Today in the United States and Canada, we favor dogs who stand tall, holding "steady to wing and shoot," and who do not drop. It's a matter of taste.

The high-tailed point is coveted by setter folks. To them, nothing matches it for canine beauty. But the high tail has a practical purpose, for often the dog can't be seen in high grass or thick cover, so the tail acts as a flag, signaling the dog's whereabouts.

Even a low tail sends a message and tells a story. For some dogs, it indicates an uncertainty, usually resulting from the dogs picking up remnant scent left by a recently departed bird, one that has run off. Setter owners read their dogs' eyes at home; in the field, they read their tails.

Another form of style merged with function is "backing," or "honoring." One dog is pointing the bird; the other dog or dogs, if trained to honor, stop hunting and slam into a sympathetic point. The hunter, perhaps unable to see exactly who is where, will follow the eyes of the honoring dogs – the ones pointing the dog that's pointing the bird. This is one reason why bird dogs are often run in pairs, or braces.

Of course, when everything works perfectly . . . well, it's about as good as it gets.

A lthough not bred to retrieve, many setters take to it naturally. In fact, some relish this important task. To them, there is the satisfaction that comes with closure on the entire drama of seeking, pointing, and finally reducing to possession. You can almost hear the dog saying, "I did it, I did it, I did it!"

A setter's drive to hunt can often place it in harm's way in the field. On warm fall days, for example, there's no such thing as too much water. Or too much mud.

A nd naturally, there are always porcupine quills, cactus spines, thorns, briars, frayed tail-tips, and the odd skunk now and then just to liven up the day – and make the ride home memorable.

The bond between setter and upland hunter is an unshakeable one, built on shared love for the places and experiences of autumn. These days afield remind both that their time together is too little, too brief.

I wonder what it is that dogs dream of, what moves them in their sleep to twitch their feet and curl their lips and whine and woof? Especially setters who have lived their lives as gun dogs; they seem to have more to dream about, maybe because they've been more places and seen and done more things worth dreaming about. Maybe it's because they gather more experience to store against these times when the season is closed or we're busy and can't take them hunting. Or when age finally makes days in the field only memories.

Puppies

Life's a Dance –
You Learn as You Go

Choosing a setter puppy from a bunch of look-alike hooligans can be daunting. Perfectly, the pup will be taken from the litter on the forty-ninth day of life – precisely seven weeks of age. Since it's difficult to tell too much about puppies at this age, supposed tests for emerging traits notwithstanding, the best bet is to choose the right litter, the right breeding, that will give you the dog you're looking for. If you want a sweet-breathed family pet with sad eyes and a gentle, pliable disposition, choose from a litter where the parents are of that persuasion. If you want a close-working hunting dog, go to a litter where both the dam and the sire hunt close. If you want a high-headed, tail-cracking bird dog that constantly digs for the horizon, you need to make sure mom and dad were poured from that mold – begging the question about how they slowed down long enough to produce all those little squirmers in the first place.

A face of guileless innocence. A brain full of shenanigans. But not to worry; the pup will outgrow its mischieviousness when it reaches maturity at a year and a half of age . . . or maybe nine or ten years after that. For now, it's those itchy teeth that get it into most trouble. Especially when they're gnawing on our things, or worse – on us.

Gracing the pup with the right name is imperative. The plan goes that getting to know his or her name will be the first step the pup takes on the long road toward learning to do what we want when we want. That's our plan, anyway. The pup may have other notions.

T hose who live with setters tend toward the romantic when picking out a moniker, preferring names such as Briar, and Misty, and Willow, and Dram.

But what we call the pup right after it eats our only good pair of black shoes right down to those little plastic things on the laces is another matter entirely. In any case, it certainly is a welcome sight to see a pup snap to attention the first time he or she recognizes that the funny sound we're making is its name.

Even as puppies, setters start to exhibit early warning signs of aristocratic arrogance and the regal bearing they will cultivate throughout their lives. These blue-bloods among canines will employ their beauty, like a lovely, overindulged child, to at once warm our hearts . . . and to get their own way.

Setters can be pointing fools. Early in life, they learn to coax their owners into convulsions of ecstasy by snapping into a stylish point at just about anything that strikes their fancy. The owner doesn't seem to care, at least at first; later on, he or she may get a little disenchanted with the whole enterprise if the dog ignores pheasants, quail, and partridge and instead makes a federal case out of pointing things like mice, butterflies, and abandoned farm equipment.

But who has a heart so dead that it won't leap at the sight of that first-ever puppy-point? They can't help it. It's their ancestors whispering in their ears.

Ah, the blessed event – a litter of setter pups. Payback time for all the hell the old girl has raised since she, herself, was a pup. Overrun by her own demanding progeny, her beseeching eyes are asking you, "How did you let this happen to me? What did I ever do to deserve this? It's not fair." But you know she'll make a fine mother, and you smile sweetly back at her and think – *heh, heh, fair?*

C ouldn't ya . . . well, come on.
Couldn't ya just love me?

I t is now that the little beast must become socialized –
humanized – indoctrinated into our way of life. There is so
much to learn, and that young, spongelike, developing brain will
assimilate it rapidly.

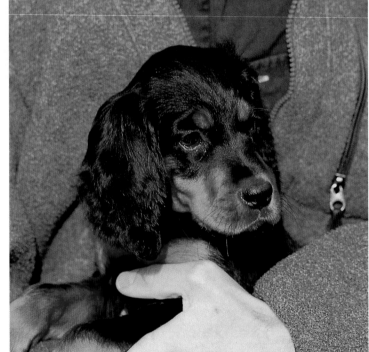

S eemingly as we watch, they grow and change. And they're watching us as well, looking for signs of what pleases us, what makes us happy, makes us want to take a few minutes for a hug or a little rough-and-tumble. Manipulative? Sure. It's the setter way.